REGISTRATION – Please Print!

AF801644

Location of the class: ______________________ Grade ______________________

Name: ____________________________________ Date: ______________________

Phone number: ________________________ Birthdate: ______________________

Ethnicity: ☐ White ☐ Latino ☐ Asian ☐ African American ☐ Native American ☐ Other __________

☐ Male ☐ Female Number of people living in your household: ______________________

Where do you get your money? Check all that apply.

☐ Work ☐ Allowance ☐ Birthday ☐ Christmas ☐ Other (please describe) ______________________

How often do you get money? ☐ Daily ☐ Weekly ☐ Monthly ☐ Other (please describe) __________

What are the top 3 things you spend money on? ______________________________

Please check yes or no:	**Yes**	**No**
Have you ever created a budget?		
Do you have a bank account?		
Do you understand price per ounce?		
Do you save money?		
Do you eat more than 5 meals a week at a fast food place or restaurant?		
Does your phone have internet?		
Do you have a washer and dryer at home?		
Do you keep write down where you spend your money?		
Do you have a plan for when you get extra money like birthday money?		
Do you get gift cards like amazon, iTunes, etc.		
Do you like to spend money?		
Do you like to save money?		

Tear this page out and give to the trainer!

Dollars 4 YOU

In God We Trust ®

Teen Workbook

Words of Wisdom (WOW) Edition

Sara Money

About the Author

Sara Money is an expert in providing a financial literacy education system for organizations who are inspired to help people who are living in survival mode (i.e. paycheck to paycheck).

- Author of eleven books on financial literacy
- MA in Counseling, 1998, *Webster University*
- BA in Psychology and Communication, 1992, *University of New Mexico (UNM)*
- Counselor, APS (*Albuquerque Public Schools)*
- City Coordinator for DVULI *(DeVos Urban Leadership Initiative)*
- Executive Director, *Love INC (In the Name of Christ) of Albuquerque*
- Clearinghouse Director*, Love INC (In the Name of Christ) of Albuquerque*
- Counselor and Residential Advisor, Job Corps
- Income Support Specialist, *New Mexico Human Services Department*
- Volunteer, *Rape Crisis Center, Shelter for Victims of Domestic Violence*, *UNM Agora Crisis Center*

And...in case you were wondering, Sara Money is her real name. She was born with it!

ISBN-13: 9780996618977

Table of Contents

A MESSAGE FROM SARA

Are you ready to learn how to manage the money you currently have OR will have some day? Learning how to make a plan for your money will help you for the rest of your life. This program will teach you how to put money into categories, how to become a smart shopper, reasons to save money and so much more!

Money impacts every part of your life:

- Where you live
- What you do for transportation
- Places you want to go
- People you want to see

Hopefully, learning simple but practical things will help you become wise about money.

The *Money & ME Program* is designed to be simple, easy to understand, and help people learn how to take control of their money and their lives. It started by developing a basic budget worksheet and activities that were practical and fun. It was originally designed for adults, and now has added a Teen Edition.

I invite you to become part of the *Money & ME Program*. The important thing to remember is for *Money & ME* to be successful you must be willing to change your own habits and ways of thinking. You were born with a special purpose. I hope you will learn how to make good choices that will impact your life for years to come.

Sara Money, Director and Developer of Money & ME

ACKNOWLEDGEMENTS

From day one, this program has been a collaboration of many people, including extensive research and focus groups. Each time the *Money & ME Program* was taught, things were added and improvements were made. Each person regardless of his / her role gave insight into the development of *Money & ME*. This program would not have happened without God's inspiration and the amazing people He brought together.

It is a pleasure and honor to thank the following people:

My family:

- My daughter, Cassie, who helped with childcare, editing, development, and teaching.
- My daughter, Emily, who inspired me to keep the *Money & ME Program* simple.
- My mom, Charlene Greenwood, for proofing worksheets, PowerPoint presentations, and curriculum, often late at night to help meet program deadlines.

Editors:

- Lauren Leggee, Love INC's Administrative Assistant, sharing insight into the low-income world, helping develop focus, and sometimes being "the focus group."
- Tori Pilcher, Love INC's Thrift Store Manager and *Money & ME* Manager, "pulling together" the many components, advising on redesign of worksheets and revising content.
- Matthew Valerio-Hirschfeld, Ph.D., professor at Trinity Southwest University, assisted with scripture references and development.
- Glenda Austin, Administrator, Registrar at Trinity Southwest University, for her insight and assistance with graphic design.
- Paula Avery, Mike Henderson, and Yvonne Lara, Love INC's Writing Club, for feedback.

Others:

- Edith Carreón for translating everything into Spanish and sharing insight into the Hispanic culture.
- Love INC Board of Directors - Robert Voss, Anthony Lovato, Kevin Johnson, Steve Denning, and Terry Dwyer for their prayers and support.
- Mickey Beisman, attorney, who gave legal advice and encouragement.
- Mike Cosgrove, Executive Director of True North Financial Ministries, for sharing his knowledge and expertise of money management principles.

MEET SOMEONE NEW!

Meeting new people and developing healthy relationships will help you and your family. It is good to get to know people. Look for someone you do not know (or do not know well) and ask the following questions. You can take notes. After you are done, you may introduce this person to other people in the class.

1. What is your name?

2. Where were you born?

3. Who is your favorite movie star and why?

4. What is your favorite season (*winter, spring, summer, fall*) and why?

5. Think of other things you can ask to get to know another person.
   Write notes to help you remember.

Think of ways that you are similar to and different from the person you talked with and write them down.

Similar	Different

Section 1: Reality Check

GETTING STARTED

The first step in gaining control of your money is to find how much money you receive each month and how much you are spending.

Step 1: When do you receive money or gift cards?

- Birthdays
- Christmas
- Working
- Allowance
- Gift cards like Amazon, itunes, Walmart, etc is considered income.

Step 2: Look for information to show how you are spending your money

- Receipts
- Bills
- Money order stubs
- Bank statements / checkbooks
- Credit report (check online for free credit reports)
- ANYTHING that shows your spending.

Step 3: Find a place to keep everything together

- Basket
- Box
- Notebook
- Receipt Organizer (*Money & ME Kit*)
- ANTHING that can help you stay organized and keep your money information.

  NOTE: If it is a gift make sure you thank that person!

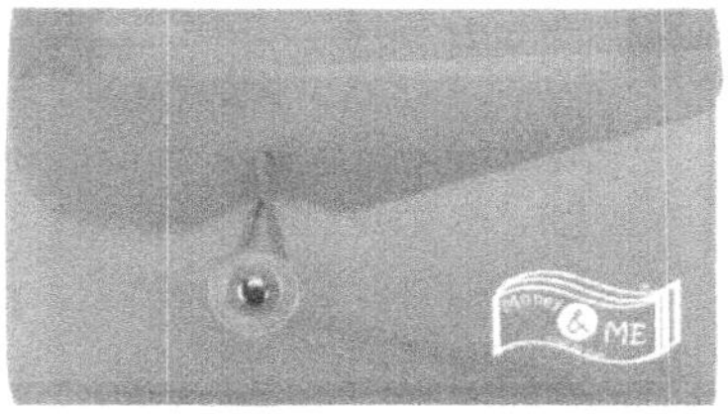

INCOME & SPENDING WORKSHEET - TEEN

INCOME	Me
Allowance	
Working	
Birthday	
Christmas	
Other	
TOTAL	

HOBBIES

Art	$ ______
Hunting/Fishing	$ ______
Photography	$ ______
Sports	$ ______
Drama	$ ______
Chess	$ ______
Cars	$ ______
Other:	$ ______
TOTAL	$ ______

FOOD

Groceries	$ ______
Eating Out	$ ______
Other:	$ ______
TOTAL	$ ______

TRANSPORTATION

Public Transportation	$ ______
Car Payment	$ ______
Gas / Oil	$ ______
Car Insurance	$ ______
Repairs / Maintenance	$ ______
Car Registration / Emissions	$ ______
Other: driver's license, etc.	$ ______
TOTAL	$ ______

FRIENDS & FAMILY

Birthday	______
Christmas	______
Other:	______
TOTAL	$ ______

SAVINGS

Emergency	$ ______
Special Purchases	$ ______
Future	$ ______
TOTAL	$ ______
	$ ______

GIVING

______

SCHOOL EXPENSES

School Supplies	______
Tuition	$ ______
School Lunch	$ ______
Activity Fees	$ ______
Other:	$ ______
TOTAL	$ ______

CLOTHING / PERSONALCARE

Clothing	$ ______
Shoes	$ ______
Laundry	$ ______
Haircuts	$ ______
Cell Phone	$ ______
Toiletries/Body Care	______
Make-up	______
Other:	$ ______
TOTAL	$ ______

ENTERTAINMENT

Movies / Rentals	$ ______
Out-of-town Trips	$ ______
Internet	$ ______
Music	$ ______
Dances	$ ______
Bowling	$ ______
Miniature Golf	$ ______
Concerts	$ ______
Games	$ ______
Other:	$ ______
TOTAL	$ ______

TOTAL MONTHLY INCOME	$ ______
TOTAL MONTHLY SPENDING	$ ______
DIFFERENCE	$ ______

INCOME & SPENDING WORKSHEET - ADULT

MONTHLY INCOME	Me	Spouse	Other Person
Paycheck (take home pay)			
Disability / Social Security $	1,000		
Food Stamps (SNAP) / WIC	100		
TANF			
Other (child support, etc.)			
TOTAL	1,100		

GIVING $ $100

HOUSING

Rent	$ 220
Mortgage	$
Gas	$ 30
Electric	$ 30
Insurance	$
Phone (landline)	$
Water / Trash / Sewer	$ 20
Other: home repairs, etc.	$
TOTAL	$ 300

FOOD / HOME SUPPLIES

Groceries	$ 100
Cleaning / Paper Supplies	$ 20
Other:	$
TOTAL	$ 120

TRANSPORTATION

Public Transportation	$
Car Payment	$
Gas / Oil	$ 40
Car Insurance	$ 20
Repairs / Maintenance	$
Car Registration / Emissions	$
Other: driver's license, etc.	$
TOTAL	$ 60

MONEY OWED to People, Rent-to-own, Student Loans, Credit Cards, Pawn Shops, etc. This amount will be filled in AFTER you complete the Payment Plan.

TOTAL $ 270

SAVINGS

Emergency	$ 25
Other:	$ 25
TOTAL	$ 50

CHILD EXPENSES

School Supplies / Activity Fees	$ 40
Childcare / Tuition	$
School Lunches	$
Allowance	$
Other:	$
TOTAL	$ 40

CLOTHING / PERSONAL ITEMS

Clothing / Shoes	$ 15
Body Care / Cosmetics	$ 15
Laundry	$ 10
Haircuts	$
Cell Phone	$ 45
Other:	$
TOTAL	$ 85

MEDICAL / DENTAL (non-emergencies)

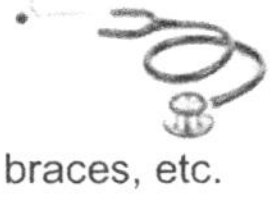

Doctor / Dentist	$
Prescriptions	$ 15
Other: insurance, glasses, braces, etc.	$
TOTAL	$ 15

EXTRA STUFF

Cable / Satellite TV	$
Movies / Rentals	$ 10
Internet	$ 10
Hobbies	$
Hobbies	$ 20
Pets	$
Gambling	$
Out–of–Town Trips	$
Birthdays / Celebrations	$ 20
Cigarettes / Alcohol	$
Other: manicures, tattoos, etc.	$
TOTAL	$ 60

TOTAL MONTHLY INCOME	$	1,100
TOTAL MONTHLY SPENDING	$	1,100
DIFFERENCE	$	0

Section 1

SAVINGS

Think about choosing some amount of money each month for savings. It is important to know WHY you are saving and how much you need to save. Answer the following questions.

1. Why should you save money each month?

2. What are things you should be saving for?

3. Some people save for an emergency. List things that you think would be good to have an emergency savings for.

4. Some people save for special purchases. Are there special things that you would like to save for?

5. Some people save for their future. What would you like to see in your future?

List things you would like to save for and how much you think you need.

SAVINGS	LIST ITEMS	TOTAL AMOUNT NEEDED
Emergency		
Special things		
Your future		
TOTAL		

HOW MUCH DO MY PARENTS SPEND ON ME?

Identify the categories where you cost your parents money. Housing, food, and transportation can be totaled and then divided by number of people in your household. Write down monthly or annual expenses. You can guess the amount and talk to you parents later to get the actual amounts. Use the Income & Spending Worksheet to help you. Multiply monthly amounts x 12 to get annual amounts.

List the shared expenses with others in your household. Divide by number in household to get your amount:	**MONTHLY AMOUNT Your Best Guess**	**MONTHLY AMOUNT Write Actual Amount**	**Annual Amount is Monthly Amount X 12. *(Use actual amount here.)***
HOUSING			
FOOD / HOME SUPPLIES			
FAMILY TRANSPORTATION			

What do my parents spend on me?!			
Medical / Dental / Braces/ Glasses			
Legal Fees			
Cell Phone			
Tuition/Books / Activity Fees			
Dorm / Apartment / Camp			
Clothes			
Car Payment			
Car Insurance			
Allowance			
Driver's Education / License			
Yearbook / Graduation Expenses			
Computer / Electronics			
Entertainment / Hobbies			
Other:			
TOTAL			

What did you learn from this activity? ____

NEEDS OR WANTS

OR

Many people think they NEED something when they actually WANT something. Think about things you NEED and things you WANT. Write them down. This will help you make better choices when you are spending your money.

Step 1: Ask yourself, "*Do you need something…**OR**…do you want something*?"

Write needs and wants in the box.

Step 2:

1. Discuss with other people what things they think are NEEDS or WANTS. ____________

    ____

2. Are you similar or different to other people? ____________

    ____

3. How could this change the way you spend money? ____________

    ____

HOW MUCH DO YOU SPEND A YEAR?

$

You may not realize how much you are spending a year on items because you buy them daily, weekly, or monthly. In this activity, write down some items you buy regularly and see how much they cost you a year. You may want to change your spending habits after you do this activity.

Look at the example to see how much these 3 items are costing a year.

How often:	Step 1: List item	Step 2: How much $	Step 3: Spent in a year
Daily	*Lunch/Snacks/Drinks*	*$7.00*	X 365 = ***$2,555***
Weekly	*Movies/Snacks*	*$20.00*	X 52 = ***$1,040***
Monthly	*Phone*	*$70.00*	X 12 = ***$840***

Step 1: Think of items you spend money on daily, weekly, and monthly - write them down.

Step 2: Write down how much the items cost.

Step 3: Figure out how much you are spending every year on these purchases.

How often:	Step 1: List item	Step 2: How much $	Step 3: Spent in a year
Daily			X 365 =
Weekly			X 52 =
Monthly			X 12 =

1. What surprised you when you realized how much money you are spending a year on an item?

____

2. Think of a person who you can share what you learned and write his or her name below. Help them identify their own spending and how much it is costing them a year.

____

Section 2: Responsibility

IMPORTANT TIPS

Develop Healthy Relationships

- Spend time with other people.
- Ask people how they are doing and listen to their responses.
- Eat meals together.
- Think of other ways to show you care about others.

Brush & Floss Your Teeth Two Times Each Day!

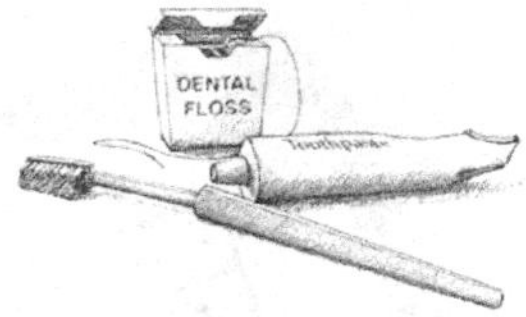

- You will be healthier and save money at the dentist.
- Encourage others (especially children) to do the same so they will have healthy teeth as adults.

Check Your Car

- Check your oil. (Have someone teach you if you don't know how.)
- Do regular oil changes and tune-ups.
- Check your tires.

Laundry Tips

- Buy the same type of socks for each child to make matching socks easier.
- Buy enough socks and underwear for each family member for at least one week.
- Teach your children, when they are old enough, to help you.
- Encourage teenagers to do their own laundry.
- Keep a jar of quarters handy so you have money to go to the laundromat.

THINGS TO DO!

Everyone has things they need to do on a *regular* basis (daily, weekly, and monthly). It could be doing dishes, getting food to eat, washing laundry, and paying your bills on time.

Think of it like a backpack. If you were going on a day trip, you would need to pack things you need for the day. You do not want to overload your backpack or it can become a burden.

Doing these things *regularly* will help you prevent them from becoming a burden to you or someone else. What things do YOU need to do on a *regular* basis? Write them down.

Daily	Weekly	Monthly
Wash dishes	*Do laundry*	*Pay bills*

1. What happens if you do not take care of things on a regular basis?

2. Has this ever happened to you?

3. Why is it important for you to take care of things regularly?

4. How will you start?

Visit www.flylady.net for new ideas on how to take care of things on a regular basis.

PLAN AHEAD

It is important for you to see how stable your income is. Whether you work or receive disability or other monthly checks it is important for you to **PLAN AHEAD** for the unexpected. This will help you become a more reliable employee.

Normal day	Unexpected
Get up	Family Emergency
Go to work	Your ride to school isn't available
Come home	You get sick

- If you have a job, answer the following questions to help you **PLAN AHEAD** for the unexpected.
- If you are a person who does not work for your income, how can you help people who have jobs?
- Discuss with other people to make sure this is a good plan.

1. What would happen if you lose your job OR someone you know loses his / her job?

____

2. If you have children and they get sick, who can take care of them while you are at work?

____

3. How do you get to work (car, bus, a friend gives a ride)? What can you do if you cannot get your regular ride?

____

4. What is your employer's policy about calling in when you get sick?

____

5. What are things you can do to stay healthy?

____

6. How important is communicating with your supervisor about your situation?

____

7. How can you encourage other people with jobs to keep their jobs?

____

8. What other things can you do to be a good employee and keep your job?

____

Don't Gossip! A negative work environment is created when people talk about others. Don't talk about people when they are not with you. If someone starts to talk to you about someone else, tell them they should talk directly to the other person. Let them know if they have a problem they need to talk about a supervisor about it. **THINK OF POSITVE THINGS TO TALK ABOUT!**

SAVER OR SPENDER?

Think about how your parents handled money. Are you similar or different? Answer the following questions to help you remember what it was like for you as a child.

1. Did your parents talk to you about money? ______________________________

2. If you had a parent who was a spender, what did he / she buy? ______________

3. If you had a parent who was a saver, what did he / she save for? ____________

4. In what ways are you like your parents? _____________________________

5. In what ways are you different from your parents? _______________________

6. Are there things you would like to change about how you handle money? _______

7. If you are a parent, what would you like your children to learn about handling money?

8. How can you teach children you know positive ways to manage the money they have or will have? ______________________________

HEALTHY or UNHEALTHY HABITS

 OR 

What is a habit? It is an automatic behavior. Everyone has habits and we need habits. It is good to be in a routine and do things automatically. Could you imagine having to think about everything you do from the time you wake up until you go to bed? Some habits are healthy, like brushing your teeth and exercising. Some habits are unhealthy like smoking and drinking. People can change habits, but it takes hard work and time.

Step 1: Write in the boxes healthy and unhealthy habits.

HEALTHY	UNHEALTHY
Brushing Teeth Exercise	Gaming Procrastination Biting finger nails

Step 2: Circle the habits above (both healthy & unhealthy) that you have.

Step 3: Answer the following questions.

1. Why do people have unhealthy habits? ______________________________
2. Why do YOU have unhealthy habits? ______________________________
3. How can stopping an unhealthy habit change your life? ______________________________
4. What would change for YOU if you stopped an unhealthy habit? ______________________________
5. What do you think keeps people from stopping an unhealthy habit? ______________________________

Section 3: Smart Shopping

SMART SHOPPING TIPS

Write down EVERYTHING you spend money on in your notepad OR in an app. When you:

- Buy a drink.
- Buy clothes.
- Buy anything!

Shop at Thrift Stores

There are lots of clothes, shoes, and accessories at lower prices than department stores.

Budget Billing

- The amount you pay for utilities can change each month which makes it difficult to budget your housing category.
- The utility company will add up how much was spent for the past year and divide by 12 to determine your monthly payment.
- This will make it a "fixed" amount which means it will be the same amount each month.

REMEMBER:

- Consider where you shop.
- Always look at price per ounce.
- Look at how items are packaged.
- Compare store brands to name brands.
- Use coupons (don't forget there are coupons on your smartphone).
- Make your own cleaning supplies.
- Shop at thrift stores to save on clothing, large purchases, and other items.
- Find out if you're eligible for "Budget Billing."

CLEANING RECIPES

Countertops, Sinks, Toilets: White Vinegar and Water

- Mix 1 cup white vinegar and 1 cup water in a spray bottle.
- Spray and scrub.
- Warm the solution first for really tough soap scum or mineral deposits. Spray the solution and let it sit before scrubbing, or use straight vinegar.

(**DO NOT USE** undiluted vinegar on tile grout – it can cause the grout to break down.)

Bathtub & Sink Scrub: Baking Soda, Squirt of Dish Soap, Lemon Juice

- Mix baking soda, a squirt of dish soap, and lemon juice in a bowl.
- Paste should be smooth like cake frosting.
- Dip a cloth or sponge into the paste and scrub.
- Rinse off paste.
- Allow the paste to sit for 10-15 minutes before rinsing for really tough stains.

Mirror & Glass Cleaner: White Vinegar and Water

- 2 teaspoons white vinegar
- 1 quart water
- Mix in a spray bottle. Spray on mirror or glass and wipe clean. You can use newspaper or coffee filters to wipe mirrors or glass.

Laundry Detergent: Soap, Washing Soda, Borax

INGREDIENTS

- 1 bar of soap
- 1 cup washing soda
- 1 cup Borax

DIRECTIONS

- Grate the ENTIRE bar of soap.
- Put grated soap and washing soda into a blender and blend.
- Pour this mixture in a bowl, add Borax and mix thoroughly.
- Store in an airtight plastic container.
- Dissolve 1 heaping tablespoon of the mixture in water before adding clothes.

Make sure to write what is in the bottle, put the date you made it, and store out of reach of children. This is so you don't forget what you have put in each bottle!

Fabric Softener, White Vinegar

- Add ½ cup white vinegar to the rinse cycle of the washing machine to help soften fabrics.
- DO NOT add at the beginning. Your clothes will smell like vinegar.
- You can also use a fabric dispenser ball.

Bonus Tip

- Cut sponges in half.
- Use half of a sponge at a time.
- Sponges will last you twice as long.

For more tips go to: www.pinterest.com and search for cleaning tips.

HEALTH TIPS

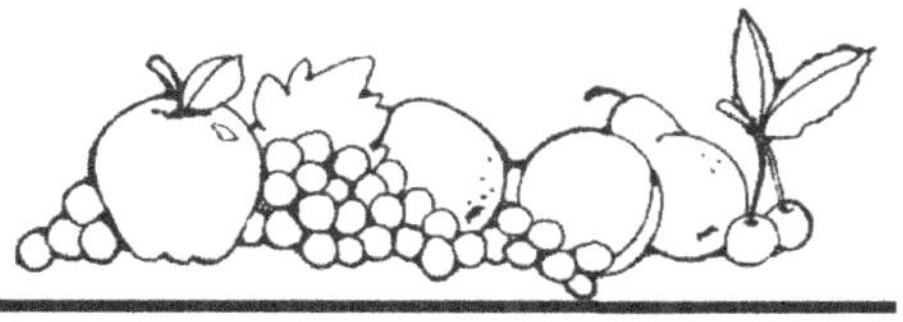

Eating Healthy

- Drink more water.
- Eat more fruits and vegetables.
- Eat less junk food. *Fruits and vegetables are more nutritious than chips.*
- Find new ways to cook at home for less money.

Low Cost Exercise

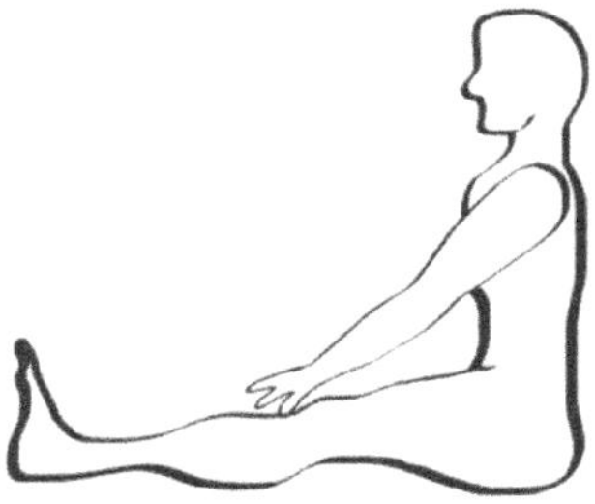

- Walking
- Hiking (Make sure you drink plenty of water.)
- Stretching
- Yoga
- Riding a bike
- Anything you can do to get exercise will make you healthier and could save you money!

MEALS FOR THE WEEK - SAMPLE

Planning your meals for the week will help you save money. This will help you stop going to the store multiple times which costs more money. This will also help you avoid eating fast food which can be very expensive.

Step 1: Think of food you and your family like to eat. Write down what you would like to eat for breakfast, lunch, snack, and dinner.

Breakfast - Cereal and milk, toast, fruit, yogurt, eggs, pancakes, etc.

Sunday	Monday	Tuesday	Wednesday	Thursday	Friday	Saturday
Eggs Toast	Cereal Fruit	French Toast	Bacon Pancakes	Oatmeal	Yogurt Fruit	Breakfast Burrito

Lunch - Hot dogs, sandwiches (*peanut butter & jelly, grilled cheese, meat)*, soup, salads, frozen meals, etc. You may have food *left over* from dinner that would be good.

Sunday	Monday	Tuesday	Wednesday	Thursday	Friday	Saturday
Ham Sandwich	Hot Dogs	Soup	Salad	Burrito	Frozen meal	Peanut Butter Sandwich

Snacks – Fruit, vegetables, yogurt, nuts, popcorn, cheese, etc. Think of healthy snacks you and your family like to eat.

Sunday	Monday	Tuesday	Wednesday	Thursday	Friday	Saturday
Fruit	Yogurt	Popcorn	Nuts	Smoothie	Crackers & Cheese	Veggies & Dip

Dinner - Tacos, hamburgers, chicken, fish, pasta, soups, casseroles, etc.

Sunday	Monday	Tuesday	Wednesday	Thursday	Friday	Saturday
Tacos	Lasagna	Casserole	Spaghetti	Fish	Chicken	Meatloaf

Step 2: Write a shopping list using your meal plan. You can use any paper for your list.
Note: There are apps you can use to help with menus and shopping lists.

MEALS FOR THE WEEK

Planning your meals for the week will help you save money. This will help you stop going to the store multiple times which costs more money. This will also help you avoid eating fast food which can be very expensive.

Step 1: Think of food you and your family like to eat. Write down what you would like to eat for breakfast, lunch, snack, and dinner.

Breakfast - Cereal and milk, toast, fruit, yogurt, eggs, pancakes, etc.						
Sunday	**Monday**	**Tuesday**	**Wednesday**	**Thursday**	**Friday**	**Saturday**

Lunch - Hot dogs, sandwiches (*peanut butter & jelly, grilled cheese, meat)*, soup, salads, frozen meals, etc. You may have food *left over* from dinner that would be good.						
Sunday	**Monday**	**Tuesday**	**Wednesday**	**Thursday**	**Friday**	**Saturday**

Snacks – Fruit, vegetables, yogurt, nuts, popcorn, cheese, etc. Think of healthy snacks you and your family like to eat.						
Sunday	**Monday**	**Tuesday**	**Wednesday**	**Thursday**	**Friday**	**Saturday**

Dinner - Tacos, hamburgers, chicken, fish, pasta, soups, casseroles, etc.						
Sunday	**Monday**	**Tuesday**	**Wednesday**	**Thursday**	**Friday**	**Saturday**

Step 2: Write a shopping list using your meal plan. You can use any paper for your list.
Note: There are apps you can use to help with menus and shopping lists.

FEELINGS AFFECT SPENDING

Many times you may be spending money because of conditions such as depression, addiction, low self-esteem, a bad habit, boredom, or you are happy! Write down your emotions, what you are buying, and how often you are purchasing items.

Emotion	What are you buying?	How often?
Sad Happy	Chips / Candy Going out to eat	Every day Every week

Relationship with money:

Think of your feelings concerning money. Check the appropriate box.

Questions	Yes	No
Are you satisfied with how you spend money?		
Are you happy when you save money?		
Are you happy when you spend money?		
Are you anxious or nervous about money?		

Be careful to not borrow money and get into a "Money Owed Trap!"

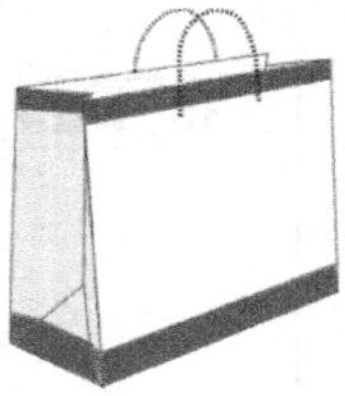

Shopping

Gaming

Snacks

Eating Out

Section 4: Money Owed Plan

MONEY FOR COLLEGE OR CAREER SCHOOLS

FINANCIAL AID CONSISTS OF THREE TYPES:

1. Scholarships – Do not have to be repaid (*Free money*)
2. Grants – Do not have to be repaid (*Free money*)
3. Student loans – HAVE TO BE REPAID PLUS INTEREST (*Not free money*)

GETTING STARTED:

- Complete FAFSA® (*Free Application for Federal Student Aid*).
- Look online for scholarships.
- Check with counselors and other academic advisors for advice.

BE AWARE OF SCAMS!

- Make sure the place you are applying for is legitimate.
- Be careful when giving your personal information including credit card numbers because criminals will use your name, social security number, and bank number(s) to obtain credit cards, set up cell phone accounts, and more.

SCHOLARSHIPS:

- There are thousands offered by schools, employers, individuals, private companies, nonprofits, communities, religious groups, and professional and social organizations.
- They are earned by meeting or exceeding certain standards set by the scholarship-giver.
- They may be specific toward particular groups of people; for instance, there are scholarships for various ethnicities, vocations, military families, etc.
- They may cover the entire cost of your tuition or it might be a one-time set award.

GRANTS:

- Amounts can change each year based on financial need, cost of attendance, and part or full-time status.
- Students may not receive *Federal Pell Grant* funds from more than one school at a time.
- The time limit of *Federal Pell Grant* funds you may receive over your lifetime is 6 years.
- There is a grant for people who want to become teachers called the TEACH Grant.

IMPORTANT INFORMATION ABOUT STUDENT LOANS

STUDENT LOANS = NOT FREE

YOU WILL HAVE TO PAY BACK STUDENT LOANS PLUS INTEREST!

Interest means paying back more money than you borrowed on your loan.

Borrow minimum amount: Loan officers may offer you more money. Do not do it! The MORE you borrow the MORE you pay back because of interest.

Grace period: You do not pay while you are taking classes. You start paying after you stop going to school. If you drop out, you still have to pay the money back.

Payments: The amount of money you have to pay starts as soon as you receive a bill.

Accountability: Make sure you pay on time and keep track of your payments. Contact the loan officer immediately if you have a problem making a payment.

Delinquent: If you miss making a payment (even by ONE day). *Consider setting up an automatic payment.*

Default: When you do not make payments, the bank or the federal government will take action to get back the money you borrowed. The consequences may include:

- You are IMMEDIATELY expected to pay the FULL amount with interest.
- You lose eligibility for repayment plans.
- You lose eligibility for additional federal student aid.
- Your loan account is assigned to a collection agency.
- Your credit rating is damaged.
- Your federal and state income taxes may be withheld.
- Your student loan debt will increase because of late fees, additional interest, court costs, collection fees, attorney fees, and any other costs associated with the collection process.
- Your employer can withhold money from your pay.
- You may have the amount of your social security reduced to pay back the loan.

BAD CREDIT WILL MAKE IT DIFFICULT TO:

- Sign up for utilities.
- Get a cell phone plan.
- Get approval to rent an apartment (credit checks are usually required for renters).
- Buy a house.

MONEY OWED LIST - ADULT SAMPLE

This worksheet will help you develop a plan to pay back the people and places you owe.

Step 1: Write down all the people and places you owe money.
Step 2: Write down the Minimum Monthly Payment.
Step 3: Write down the Total Amount Owed (Interest & Fees).
Step 4: Rank the smallest with the number "1." Continue ranking the "Rank Total Amount Owed" column from the smallest to largest using the Total Amount Owed.

Category	**Step 1:** List of People and Places Money Owed	**Step 2** Minimum Monthly Payment	**Step 3:** Total Amount Owed (Interest & Fees)	**Step 4:** Rank "Total Amount Owed" from smallest to largest
MONEY OWED: People, Rent-to-own, Credit Cards, Pawn Shops, Student Loans, Medical Bills *(not monthly)*, Child Support, Taxes, Other:	*Medical Bills*	*$60*	*$7,000*	
	Family Member	*$50*	*$600*	
	Rent-to-own	*$60*	*$6,000*	
	Student Loan	*$60*	*$4,500*	
	Pawn Shop	*$40*	*$80*	
TOTAL of Minimum Monthly Payments				
TOTAL Amount Owed				

Income & Spending Worksheet and Monthly Budget Worksheet

MONEY OWED LIST

This worksheet will help you develop a plan to pay back the people and places you owe.

Step 1: Write down all the people and places you owe money.
Step 2: Write down the Minimum Monthly Payment.
Step 3: Write down the Total Amount Owed (Interest & Fees).
Step 4: Rank the smallest with the number "1." Continue ranking the "Rank Total Amount Owed" column from the smallest to largest using the Total Amount Owed.

Category	**Step 1:** List of People and Places Money Owed	**Step 2** Minimum Monthly Payment	**Step 3:** Total Amount Owed (Interest & Fees)	**Step 4:** Rank "Total Amount Owed" from smallest to largest
MONEY OWED: People Rent-to-own Credit Cards Pawn Shops Student Loans Medical Bills *(not-monthly)* Child Support Taxes Other:				
TOTAL of Minimum Monthly Payments				
TOTAL Amount Owed				

Income & Spending Worksheet and Monthly Budget Worksheet

PAYMENT PLAN – ADULT SAMPLE

It is important to develop a plan to pay back people and places you owe money. Follow the steps below to help you create a Payment Plan.

Step 1: Look at your Money Owed List. Look at the People and Places Owed Money column. Which one ranked #1?

Step 2: Re-write that information on the Payment Plan, beginning with #1.

Step 3: Continue with #2 ranking, then #3, and so on until the Payment Plan is completed.

Ranking of Total Amount Owed Smallest to Largest	People and Places Owed Money	Total Amount Owed (Interest & Fees)	Monthly Payment
1.	Pawn Shop	$80	$40
2.	Family Member	$600	$50
3.	Student Loan	$4,500	$60
4.	Rent-to-own	$6,000	$60
5.	Medical Bills	$7,000	$60
6.			
7.			
8.			
9.			
10.			

Note: Be patient! This might take a long time. When you have paid off the money owed, you can now put money toward savings and / or reward your family!

PAYMENT PLAN

It is important to develop a plan to pay back people and places you owe money. Follow the steps below to help you create a Payment Plan.

Step 1: Look at your Money Owed List. Look at the People and Places Owed Money column. Which one ranked #1?

Step 2: Re-write that information on the Payment Plan, beginning with #1.

Step 3: Continue with #2 ranking, then #3, and so on until the Payment Plan is completed.

Ranking of Total Amount Owed Smallest to Largest	People and Places Owed Money	Total Amount Owed (Interest & Fees)	Monthly Payment
1.			
2.			
3.			
4.			
5.			
6.			
7.			
8.			
9.			
10.			

Note: Be patient! This might take a long time. When you have paid off the money owed, you can now put money toward savings and / or reward your family!

EXTRA MONEY PLAN -- SAMPLE

Sometimes you may receive extra income (taxes, gift, or inheritance). You need to make a plan for this extra money.

Questions to ask:

What percentage do I want to give (non-profit organizations)? *10%*

What percentage do I want to pay toward money owed? *60%*

What percentage do I want to put toward my savings? *10%*

What percentage do I want to use for helping others in need (family and friends)? *10%*

What percentage do I want to spend on extra stuff? *10%*

USE A PENCIL

Make a plan for any **extra money.** Use your calculator to figure out the percentage. When you do get extra money, you can use this as a guideline. If you need help, contact your *Money & ME* Coach or the facility that hosted the *Money & ME Program*.

TOTAL Amount Extra Money	Category	Multiply total by % You decide how much	Amount for each category to put into envelope	Figure out how much you want each "piece of the pie" to have? This is a percentage. Some pieces will be larger than others.
$1,000	*Giving*	*10%*	*=$100*	
	Money Owed	*60%*	*=$600*	
	Savings	*10%*	*=$100*	
	Others	*10%*	*=$100*	
	Extra Stuff	*10%*	*=$100*	
		100% *This should equal 100%*	*$1,000* *(This should equal the TOTAL Amount)*	

EXTRA MONEY PLAN

Sometimes you may receive extra income (taxes, gift, or inheritance). You need to make a plan for this extra money.

Questions to ask:

What percentage do I want to give (non-profit organizations)?________________________________

What percentage do I want to pay toward money owed? ________________________________

What percentage do I want to put toward my savings? ________________________________

What percentage do I want to use for helping others in need (family and friends)?______________

What percentage do I want to spend on extra stuff? ________________________________

USE A PENCIL

Make a plan for any **extra money.** Use your calculator to figure out the percentage. When you do get extra money, you can use this as a guideline. If you need help, contact your *Money & ME* Coach or the facility that hosted the *Money & ME Program.*

TOTAL Amount Extra Money	Category	Multiply total by % You decide how much	Amount for each category to put into envelope	Figure out how much you want each "piece of the pie" to have? This is a percentage. Some pieces will be larger than others.
$	*Giving*	%	=$	
	Money Owed	%	=$	
	Savings	%	=$	
	Others	%	=$	
	Extra Stuff	%	=$	
		100% *This should equal 100%*	$ *This should equal the TOTAL Amount*	

BOUNDARIES

Sometimes people spend money because they have poor boundaries. A person will buy something he or she cannot afford to feel better. A person will give money because he or she fears a negative reaction which could be withdrawal of love or an angry response. Other people may ask for money and use guilt when a friend or family member doesn't give money. Answer the following questions to see if you struggle with boundaries.

Do you buy things even though you know you cannot afford them?	Yes	No
Do you give money to people when they ask? (friends, family, strangers)	Yes	No
Do you have a hard time saying "NO" to others?	Yes	No
Do you fear loss of love if you do not do things that other people want?	Yes	No
Do you think others will get angry with you if you do not do what they want?	Yes	No
Do you ask others for money?	Yes	No
Do you respect other people's boundaries when they say "NO" to you?	Yes	No
Do you punish others if they do not do what you want?	Yes	No
Do you spend money on others so you can be liked or loved?	Yes	No
Do you feel you might have a problem with boundaries?	Yes	No

Boundaries are built. You need to work on developing the ability to:

- Say "NO" to yourself.
- Say "NO" to others.
- Respect another person when they say "NO."

How to start:

Identify your feelings. Feelings tell us when something is not right. We should listen to our feelings. However, it is important to not be controlled by your feelings.

Talk to other people. Identify people you trust and let them know that you struggle with healthy boundaries. Develop healthy relationships with others.

Practice. Start setting small boundaries and practicing with people who love you and respect you for who you are. The more you practice, the easier it will become over time.

Get help. There are lots of books, information on the internet, and support groups available. A great book to get started is BOUNDARIES: (When to Say YES When to Say NO To Take Control of Your Life) by Dr. Henry Cloud and Dr. John Townsend.

Discussion Questions: Think of yourself or someone you know who has poor boundaries.

Describe the behaviors that you see that are causing problems related to money.

What advice would you give yourself or someone else who has boundary problems?

Section 5: Build a Budget

INCOME & BILLS CALENDAR - SAMPLE

Paying your bills on time will help you gain control over your finances and lighten the load of paying late fees. You can use the calendar below as a "Master Calendar" to know when your income is received and your bills are due each month. If you have a phone with a calendar, you can use the calendar app and set up reminders.

Step 1: CREATE A CALENDAR - Write in the month, year, and dates of the current month OR if it is near the end of the month – write the next month's information. Dates are to be written in the small boxes.

MONTH December **YEAR** 2019

	SUNDAY	MONDAY	TUESDAY	WEDNESDAY	THURSDAY	FRIDAY	SATURDAY
Week 1		1 Income $500	2 Water $20	3	4	5 Rent $220	6
Week 2	7	8 Pawn Shop $40	9 Gas $30 Electric $30	10	11	12 Received Food Stamps $100	13
Week 3	14	15 Income $500	16	17	18	19	20 Prescription $15
Week 4	21	22 Phone $45	23 Family Member $50	24 Student Loan $60	25 Rent-to-own $60	26 Medical Bills $60	27
Extra	28	29	30	31			

Step 2: FILL IN

- When you get paid: daily, weekly, every two weeks, monthly.
- When your bills are due.
- Write down non-monthly bills in the boxes below and on your calendar.

Non-monthly bills: These are things that do not happen every month like car registration, taxes, etc.

Income / Bills	Month & Date	$ Amount	Notes

INCOME & BILLS CALENDAR

Paying your bills on time will help you gain control over your finances and lighten the load of paying late fees. You can use the calendar below as a "Master Calendar" to know when your income is received and your bills are due each month. If you have a phone with a calendar, you can use the calendar app and set up reminders.

Step 1: CREATE A CALENDAR - Write in the month, year, and dates of the current month OR if it is near the end of the month – write the next month's information. Dates are to be written in the small boxes.

MONTH ______________________ **YEAR** ____________________

	SUNDAY	MONDAY	TUESDAY	WEDNESDAY	THURSDAY	FRIDAY	SATURDAY
Week 1							
Week 2							
Week 3							
Week 4							
Extra							

Step 2: FILL IN

- When you get paid: daily, weekly, every two weeks, monthly.
- When your bills are due.
- Write down non-monthly bills in the boxes below and on your calendar.

Non-monthly bills: These are things that do not happen every month like car registration, taxes, etc.

Income / Bills	Month & Date	$ Amount	Notes

MONTHLY BUDGET – ADULT SAMPLE

Big Bucket *Income* = Spending Categories *Expenses*

A plan for YOUR money!

Step 1: Write down each time you or a family member in your home receives money.
Step 2: Decide how much will go into each spending category. *Use your Income & Spending Worksheet to help you.* Write it down. Total all the spending.
Step 3: Subtract spending categories from the income. It should equal zero. Make changes if needed.

MONTHLY INCOME RECEIVED	Check #1	Check #2	Check #3	Check #4	Extra Money	Monthly Total	Annual Total (Monthly x 12)
Cash, check, or food stamps $	500	Food Stamps 100	500			1,100	13,200
SPENDING CATEGORIES (Start with needs)							
Housing $	300					$300	3,600
Food / Home Supplies $		100	20			$120	1,440
Clothing / Personal Items $	10		75			$85	1,020
Transportation $	40		20			$60	720
Money Owed $	40		230			$270	3,240
Child Expenses $	20		20			$40	480
Medical / Dental $			15			$15	180
Savings $	25		25			$50	600
Giving $	50		50			$100	1,200
Extra Stuff $	15		45			$60	720
TOTAL SPENDING $	500	100	500			$1100	13,200
Income subtract spending TOTAL should = 0 $	0	0	0				0

MONTHLY BUDGET - ADULT

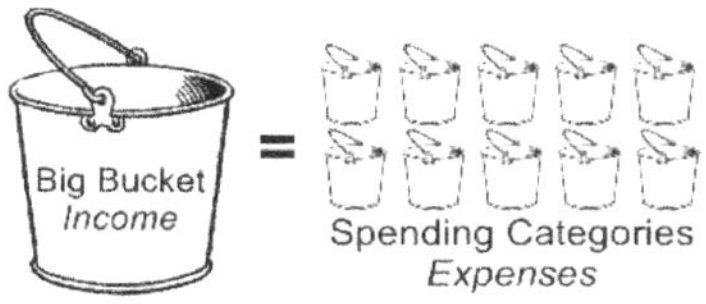

A plan for YOUR money!

Step 1: Write down each time you or a family member in your home receives money.
Step 2: Decide how much will go into each spending category. *Use your Income & Spending Worksheet to help you.* Write it down. Total all the spending.
Step 3: Subtract spending categories from the income. It should equal zero. Make changes if needed.

MONTHLY INCOME RECEIVED	Check #1	Check #2	Check #3	Check #4	Extra Money	Monthly Total	Annual Total (Monthly x 12)
Cash, check, or food stamps $							
SPENDING CATEGORIES (Start with needs)							
Housing $							
Food / Home Supplies $							
Clothing / Personal Items $							
Transportation $							
Money Owed $							
Child Expenses $							
Medical / Dental $							
Savings $							
Giving $							
Extra Stuff $							
TOTAL SPENDING $							

MONTHLY BUDGET - TEEN

A plan for YOUR money!

Step 1: Write down each time you or a family member in your home receives money.
Step 2: Decide how much will go into each spending category. *Use your Income & Spending Worksheet to help you.* Write it down. Total all the spending.
Step 3: Subtract spending categories from the income. It should zero. Make changes if needed.

MONTHLY INCOME RECEIVED	Check #1	Check #2	Check #3	Check #4	Extra Money	Monthly Total	Annual Total (Monthly x 12)
Cash, check, or food stamps $							
SPENDING CATEGORIES (Start with needs)							
Giving $							
Hobbies $							
Food $							
Transportation $							
Friends & Family $							
Savings $							
School Expenses $							
Clothing / Personal items $							
Toiletries $							
Entertainment $							
TOTAL SPENDING $							
Income subtract spending TOTAL should = 0 $							

CASH ENVELOPE SYSTEM

Using envelopes to keep your money in categories will help you stay in control of your Monthly Budget. You will write each spending category on the outside of each envelope. On the inside of each envelope you will write a word or words to help remind you what to say to yourself when the envelope is empty. For example, when the "Extra Stuff" envelope is empty, you will need to say **NO** until you get more money.

Step 1: Label envelopes

- Start with ten envelopes.
- Use the list below to label your envelopes.
- Write the category on the **outside** of the envelope (*front or back*) and the phrase on the **inside** of the envelope.

Outside of envelope	Inside of envelope
Giving	*Good Job!*
Hobbies	*No*
Food	*No*
Transportation	*No*
Friends & Family	*Good Job!*
Savings	*Good Job!*
School Expenses	*No*
Clothing / Personal Items	*No*
Toiletries	*No*
Extra Stuff	*NO!*

Step 2: Using envelopes:

- Put cash in each envelope to match the amount on your Monthly Budget.
- When shopping, take the appropriate envelope with you. Do not take all your cash!
- Purchase the item and get a receipt.
- Put paper change and receipt back in the envelope.
- Save loose change in a jar. This could be your laundry money.

Note: You can get more envelopes for more categories. For example, birthdays, Christmas, special purchases, etc. Do not get too many envelopes or it will become confusing and difficult. **Using the envelopes will help you make good money choices.**

SPENDING RECORD BY CATEGORY - SAMPLE

This worksheet will help you know how much you have in a spending category so you don't overspend. If you are using the Cash Envelope System, it should match what is in each envelope.
This is very important if you use a checkbook or EBT Card so you don't overspend in a category. There is one worksheet for each of the ten categories.

Step 1: Each time you get paid, write down the date and the amount in the "Money In" column.
Step 2: Use your Income & Spending Worksheet to see all the items related to each category.
Step 3: Each time you spend money write the date, person or place money spent, and the amount in the "Money Out" column.
Step 4: Subtract each time you spend money so you know how much you have in the category.

Spending Category	Monthly Amount Needed	Amount from Check #1	Amount from Check #2	Amount from Check #3	Amount from Check #4	Extra
Housing	*$300*	*$ 300*				

Date	Person or Place Money Spent	Money Out	Money In	Amount Left
10/1	*Money In*		*$300*	*$300*
10/2	*Water*	*$20*		*$280*
10/5	*Rent*	*$220*		*$60*
10/9	*Gas / Electric*	*$60*		*$0*
11/1	*Money In*		*$300*	*$300*
11/2	*Water*	*$20*		*$280*

You can use regular notebook paper or a smartphone budget app.

SPENDING RECORD BY CATEGORY

This worksheet will help you know how much you have in a spending category so you don't overspend. If you are using the Cash Envelope System, it should match what is in each envelope.
This is very important if you use a checkbook or EBT Card so you don't overspend in a category. There is one worksheet for each of the ten categories.

Step 1: Each time you get paid, write down the date and the amount in the "Money In" column.
Step 2: Use your Income & Spending Worksheet to see all the items related to each category.
Step 3: Each time you spend money write the date, person or place money spent, and the amount in the "Money Out" column.
Step 4: Subtract each time you spend money so you know how much you have in the category.

Spending Category	Monthly Amount Needed	Amount from Check #1	Amount from Check #2	Amount from Check #3	Amount from Check #4	Extra

Date	Person or Place Money Spent	Money Out	Money In	Amount Left

You can use regular notebook paper or a smartphone budget app.

Section 6: Take Control

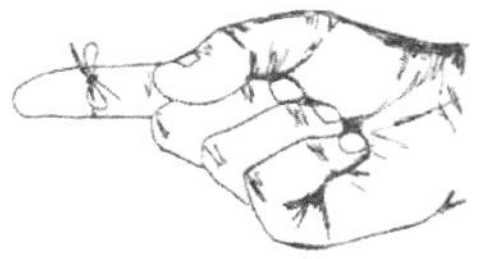

I CAN CHANGE!

What is ONE habit YOU would like to change? ______________________________

Why do YOU want to change? ______________________________
It is important to write down WHY you want to change. It could be to save money, to get healthy, for your family, for a job.

Who can help you?______________________________
Having a person to encourage you will help. Think of a family member, a friend, or a neighbor - ANYONE who can help you. Talk to this person about the habit you are going to change.

When do you want to start? ______________________________
Changing a habit is not easy. Look at your calendar and choose a day when you are going to start.

Signals to change:______________________________
Everyone has signals connected to habits. It could be a person, place, a time of day or feelings. For example, if you smoke when you are drinking, can you stop drinking if you continue to smoke?

NEW habit: ______________________________
It is important to find a healthy habit to replace the unhealthy habit. Can you chew gum, candy, or toothpicks to stop smoking?

Extra help:______________________________
Talk to a doctor or counselor, find a support group, check the internet for ideas, or get a new app for your phone. You can ask people in the organization hosting this workshop for help.

Be creative:______________________________
Do you like to create songs or artwork? Create something that will inspire you to change.

New saying:______________________________
*Change how you think by changing what you say. For example, instead of saying, "I am a smoker" change it to "**I am a non-smoker**."*

Helpful Hints – Many people go back to an unhealthy habit when they are:

- **Thirsty or Hungry** – *Drink lots of water and eat regular, healthy meals.*
- **Tired** – *Get plenty of rest! It is hard to change a behavior when you are tired.*
- **Upset** – *Create a healthy plan for when you're upset. Write out your plan to help you remember. Who can you call? What will you do? (talk to a friend, go for a walk). It is common when you are upset to go back to your unhealthy habit. Do what is on your plan instead.*

Celebrate success! ______________________________
Plan something when you have been successful for 30, 60, and 90 days. It can be simple and not cost money, but you will have a reason to celebrate your success!

Pray and Meditation: Ask God to help you change.

FUN ACTIVITIES - SAMPLE

What are things you can do with your spouse, friends, and family that do not cost a lot of money?

Step 1: Write the ideas in the boxes below.
Step 2: Use scissors to cut out the paper boxes.
Step 3: Put the paper pieces in a container (jar, cup, box, etc.)
Step 4: Have someone choose a piece of paper out of the container.
Step 5: Go have some low-cost fun!

Play card games	Find shapes in the clouds
Charades – get an app from smartphone	Bake a cake - eat it without a fork
Blowing bubbles	Go to a playground
Look at the stars	Have a picnic at a park
Play ball or Frisbee	Create an obstacle course
Water gun fight	Watch the sunrise OR sunset
Feed the birds	Go to a library
Read a book	Color / Do a craft
Dance	Build a fort with pillows & blankets
Play hide & seek OR tag	Sing Songs

Section 6

FUN ACTIVITIES

What are things you can do with your spouse, friends, and family that do not cost a lot of money?

Step 1: Write the ideas in the boxes below.
Step 2: Use scissors to cut out the paper boxes.
Step 3: Put the paper pieces in a container (jar, cup, box, etc.)
Step 4: Have someone choose a piece of paper out of the container.
Step 5: Go have some low-cost fun!

OTHER WAYS TO BE SUCCESSFUL

Most of the time, when we think of success, we usually think of money. However, there are other types of success. You don't have to have money to be successful.

Relational Success: How are your relationships with…

- Friends
- Family
- Neighbors

What are things you can do to improve your relationships?

Influential Success: Everyone is good or bad for others...

- Do you encourage others?
- Do others enjoy being with you? **OR**
- Are you negative?

What are things you can change about yourself to be a positive influence for people you are around?

Spiritual Success: What are you doing for your spiritual self…

- Who do you spend time with?
- What books do you read?
- What type of music do you listen to?
- Do you spend time in meditation or prayer?

What are things you can do to improve yourself spiritually?

Section 7: Wisdom

WISDOM

A plan for you: 

There is a plan for your life. Do your plans include a way to prosper you and your family which will not bring harm to your family? Do your plans give you and your family hope for the future?

Teaching your children:

Teach your children the proper way to live, so when they grow old, they will still walk in it.

Giving:

As the community, has provided for you, you should give back to your community.

When you give, it is good to do it with a cheerful heart.

Savings:

We should all be like the ant who works hard all summer gathering food and provisions, so when winter comes he has all that he needs.

Needs OR wants:

No one can serve both their needs and their wants. If they serve their wants, then their needs will suffer.

It is important to help someone who is experiencing  *something like a natural disaster in their life. However, it is important for you to take care of regular things like paying bills, doing laundry, and buying food so you do not become a burden (or heavy load) on other people.*

Dealing with burdens:

Work on developing relationships for people to help you, so you have support when you are experiencing a burden.

We were created to work:

It is good for people to work.

Giving: *God loves a cheerful giver.* 2 Corinthians 9:7b (HCSB)

WISDOM

Gambling:

Gambling may increase your wealth and hope for a short time, but if you put the same money in savings it will be there for the future.

Time: 

There is enough time in every day to get things done. It can be wasted in unproductive things or used to achieve the things that need to be done.

Feelings Affect Spending:

You have been remarkably and wonderfully made. Spending money will not help you feel better about yourself. It will actually make you feel worse. It is like money going down the drain.

Teach yourself and children:

People will face trials in their lives. However, if you accept the trial it will make you a stronger and better person.

Money Owed:

Wise people carefully consider taking out a loan because they understand what they have can be taken away if payments are not made.

When you borrow money from friends or family it affects the relationship.

Be thankful:

Give thanks in everything,

I can change my habits:

People who can be taught can have a better life. Those who ignore teaching will repeat their mistakes.

Volunteer: *It is more fulfilling to give to someone else than it is to get something for yourself.*

WISDOM

Other ways to be successful:

Those who love money will never have enough. Wealth does not bring true happiness!

Relational Success:

Think of things you can do to have positive, healthy relationships.

Influential Success:

Everyone is a good or bad influence on others. Think of ways you can be a positive influence on other people.

Spiritual Success: How are you spiritually?

You are not a human on a spiritual journey, you are a spirit on a human journey.

What's important:

Strive for the life that you were created for.

Section 8: Information

RESOURCES

Organizing and cleaning your home: www.flylady.net

Putting together outfits to look your best: www.missussmartypants.com

Cleaning recipes, decorating, outfits, and more: www.pinterest.com

Credit Scores: www.creditkarma.com

Free things to do: www.mrfreestuff.com

- Call museums to see if they have a free day.
- Find library activities.
- Go to parks.

NOTE: Put in the city where you are looking for free stuff to do.

Internet: Comcast for $9.95 / month - you must meet criteria listed below.

- Be located where Comcast offers Internet service.
- Have at least one child receiving free school lunches through the National School Lunch Program.
- Have not subscribed to Comcast Internet service within the last 90 days.
- Have no overdue Comcast bills or unreturned equipment.

Call 1-855-846-8376.

Housing: www.habitat.org

Habitat for Humanity is an organization that helps low-income people purchase affordable homes.

Pay off money Owed: Debt Reduction

ClearPoint: www.Credibility.org OR 1-800-251-2227
Trinity Debt Management: www.trinitycredit.org OR 1-800-758-3844

Share success stories:

When you change a habit, pay off money owed, start savings or something else, e-mail **Info@moneyandme.cash** to share YOUR success or post on the *Money & ME* Facebook page!

FOLLOW-UP: To be Done with a *Money & ME* Coach

It is helpful to meet with someone individually after you have completed *Money & ME*. Let the Trainer know you would like to meet with a Coach.

Here is a checklist for you **and** your Coach to use when reviewing your *Money & ME Workbook*. It is a good way to see what you have done and areas where you might need help.

Topic	Understands Well	Needs More Help	Notes
Income & Spending Worksheet			
Savings			
Needs OR Wants			
How Much Do You Spend in a Year?			
Things to Do!			
Plan Ahead			
Saver or Spender?			
Healthy & Unhealthy Habits			
Meals for the Week			
Feelings Affect Spending			
Income & Bills Calendar			
Monthly Budget			
Cash Envelope System			
Spending Record by Category			
Money Owed List & Payment Plan			
Boundaries			
Extra Money Plan			
I Can Change			
Other Ways to be Successful			
Scripture			

Additional questions to discuss:

1. Why is it good to save?
2. What is your emergency savings goal? How will you start?
3. What is the difference between needs and wants? How can you tell the difference?
4. How are you doing talking about money with your family or trustworthy person?
5. What are things you need to take care of daily (remember the *backpack from orientation - your own load*) so they do not become burdensome?
6. Are you using the Cash Envelope System? If yes, is it working? If no, can we talk about it and see if there are things you can do to make it work better?
7. What habit are you trying to change and how is it going?
8. Do you owe money? Do you have a Payment Plan and how is it going?
9. Which scripture has been most helpful?
10. Would you like to meet again?

TEST (Two pages – Front and Back)

Name ______________________________ Date ____________________

1. Who should make a budget?

a. Adults

b. Everyone who receives money

c. Bankers

d. All of the above

2. What is income?

a. Birthday money including gift cards

b. Money received for working

c. Holiday gifts

d. All of the above

3. What does a person NEED to spend money on?

a. Electronics

b. Food

c. Entertainment

d. Designer clothes

4. Why is looking at price per ounce important?

a. It is the best way to know you are getting a good buy

b. Smaller items can actually cost more even though the purchase price is less

c. It is a good way to be a smart shopper

d. All of the above

5. What is difference between a "want" and a "need"?

a. There is no difference, when a person wants something, it is a need

b. A "want" is something you can live without

c. A "need" is something you cannot live without

d. Both b and c

6. Can coupons save you money?

a. Yes

b. No

7. Why is it important to be responsible?

a. It promotes healthy relationships

b. So it does not stress others

c. So that you have good credit

d. All of the above

8. What is a good habit?

a. Doing daily responsibilities

b. Going to the mall

c. Buying needed items when they are on sale

d. Both a and c

9. How does buying something every day effect a person's budget?

a. It does not have any effect

b. A person spends more than they realize

c. It is makes it harder to save for something that costs more

d. Both b and c

10. Why should a person save money?

a. Emergencies

b. Education

c. Special purchases

d. All of the above

11. What items can you buy at a thrift store?

a. Clothes, athletic equipment

b. Furniture, books, home decor

c. Toys and movies

d. All of the above

12. **Which is the easiest?**

a. To borrow money

b. To pay back money to people and places

13. **What happens when you don't pay back student loans?**

a. Nothing happens

b. Bad credit which makes it difficult to get an apartment or a cell phone

c. Money can be taken out of income tax refund checks

d. Both b and c

14. **What is a budget?**

a. A plan for your money

b. A tool to help budget for categories

c. Both of the above

15. **What feelings can affect your spending?**

a. Sadness

b. Happiness

c. Boredom

d. All of the above

16. **What is good debt?**

a. A good sale on electronics

b. Purchasing something that will increase in value

c. Education expenses that will help you get a better paying job

d. Both b and c

17. **How to create a "plan for extra money?"**

a. Ask questions about what is important

b. Make decisions before you get extra money

c. Write down a prioritized list

d. All of the above

18. **When should you change a budget?**

a. When your income increases

b. A change in your family situation

c. When your income decreases

d. All of the above

19. **Why is it important to know how you spend money?**

a. So you can buy important things

b. To have awareness of how much you are spending.

c. To tell your friends how much you are able to spend on certain items.

d. All of the above

20. **Which one is NOT "free money" for education?**

a. Grants

b. Scholarships

c. Student loans

21. **How does the cash envelope system work?**

a. A place to store your money

b. A plan to not overspend in a category

c. A way to show when you are out of money

d. All of the above c

22. **What are reasons to use a calendar**

a. To keep track of appointments

b. To turn in assignments

c. To pay bills on time

d. All of the above

23. **What scams are on the internet?**

a. Websites wanting your personal information

b. Websites making a promise "to good to be true"

c. Websites pretending to be official websites

d. All of the above

24. **What does it mean when you are charged "interest"?**

a. It means someone likes me

b. Paying back more money than you borrowed on your loan

c. A Facebook like

d. None of the above

Made in United States
North Haven, CT
05 November 2026

21763946R00043